How Do You Live There?

LIVING AT HIGH ALTITUDES

Joanne Mattern

PowerKiDS
press.

NEW YORK

Published in 2021 by The Rosen Publishing Group, Inc.
29 East 21st Street, New York, NY 10010

Editor: Kristen Susienka
Designer: Rachel Rising

Photo Credits: Cover, Dennis Wegewijs/Shutterstock.com; Back Cover, pp. 3,4,6,7,8,10,12,14,16,18,20,21,22,23, 24,26,28,29,30,31,32 (background) Yevhenii Borshosh/Shutterstock.com; p. 5 Taras Kushnir/Shutterstock.com; p. 7 Denis Burdin/Shutterstock.com; p. 9 Bella Bender/Shutterstock.com; p. 11 Jonathan Byrne/Shutterstock.com; p. 13 David Varga/Shutterstock.com; p. 14 Daniel Prudek/Shutterstock.com; p. 15 R.M. Nunes/Shutterstock.com; p. 17 timurtazz/Shutterstock.com; p. 19 cge2010/Shutterstock.com; p. 21 Kris Wiktor/Shutterstock.com; p. 22 Ricardo Pacheco/Shutterstock.com; p. 23 streetflash/Shutterstock.com; p. 25 samoshkin/Shutterstock.com; p. 27 Tappasan Phurisamrit/Shutterstock.com; p. 29 Lysogor Roman/Shutterstock.com.

Library of Congress Cataloging-in-Publication Data

Names: Mattern, Joanne, 1963- author.
Title: Living at high altitudes / Joanne Mattern.
Description: New York : PowerKids Press, [2021] | Series: How do you live
   there?! | Includes bibliographical references and index.
Identifiers: LCCN 2019045459 | ISBN 9781725316485 (paperback) | ISBN
   9781725316508 (library binding) | ISBN 9781725316492 |
Subjects: LCSH: Altitude, Influence of--Juvenile literature. |
   Technological innovations--Juvenile literature.
Classification: LCC QP82.2.A4 M28 2021 | DDC 616.9/893--dc23
LC record available at https://lccn.loc.gov/2019045459

Find us on

CONTENTS

WHAT IS ALTITUDE?

Our planet has many high places. These high places have high **altitudes**. Any thing, like a mountain, a house on a hill, or a person climbing, has altitude. A place is considered to be at a high altitude if it is 6,500 feet (1,980 meters) or more above sea level.

"Sea level" means the surface of the ocean. Places that are at sea level, like an ocean beach, are said to have zero altitude. As land moves away from the ocean, it tends to increase in altitude.

Some places are thought of as very flat. They don't have many mountains. But even these places have an altitude when compared to sea level. For example, the average altitude of the U.S. state of Kansas is about 2,000 feet (610 m) above sea level.

The higher you climb on a mountain, the higher your altitude is.

HIGH PLACES AROUND THE WORLD

Many of the world's highest places are in Asia. This continent has lots of mountain **ranges**. One of these ranges is the Himalayas. This mountain range has more than 110 **peaks** that are over 24,000 feet (7,315 m) tall. Mount Everest is the highest peak in the world. It rises 29,035 feet (8,850 m) above sea level.

Many high mountains are also found in South America, North America, Africa, and Europe. The Andes Mountains in South America are very tall. So are the Rocky Mountains in North America and the Ethiopian Highlands in Africa.

Australia has the lowest altitude of any continent. Its tallest mountain, Mount Kosciuszko, is only 7,310 feet (2,228 m) tall. Antarctica, on the other hand, has an average altitude of 8,200 feet (2,500 m).

Antarctica has the highest average altitude of any continent and is home to many tall mountains.

Antarctica's Altitude

The world's tallest mountains may be in Asia, but Antarctica has the highest average altitude of any continent: 8,200 feet (2,500 m). The highest mountain there is Mount Vinson. It has a height of 16,050 feet (4,892 m). It is part of the Sentinel Range and is one of the Seven Summits of the world.

A DIFFERENT LANDSCAPE

High places like the Rocky Mountains or Mount Everest are mostly rocks covered with snow. It's cold all the time at the tops of high mountains, so the snow never melts. Trees can't grow at the tops of these peaks. Only certain plants, such as special grasses and mosses, can grow at high altitudes.

The edge of where trees can grow is called the tree line. Tree lines are at different altitudes in different places. The tree line depends on weather conditions. If it's too cold or snowy, trees can't grow. The tree line in Mexico is about 13,000 feet (3,960 m) high. In the Teton Mountains of Wyoming, where it's colder, the tree line is much lower. It's about 10,000 feet (3,050 m) high.

Mount Everest

Mount Everest is the highest place on Earth. Animals, plants, and people live lower down on the mountain. The higher you travel, the less life you find. Thousands of people have tried to climb Mount Everest. They're helped by people called Sherpas, who live in the Himalayas. Sherpas are used to Mount Everest's altitude and are good guides.

The tree line is the altitude on a mountain where trees stop being able to grow.

HIGH-ALTITUDE CHALLENGES

Life at high altitudes can be hard. However, people and animals have learned how to survive at such great heights. Yaks can live in the Himalayas because their thick fur keeps them warm. Some people live at high altitudes all the time. Others just come to visit.

It's especially difficult for visitors to get used to high altitudes. Their bodies need to **adapt** to the different environment. Until this happens, people can suffer from something called altitude sickness. They might feel tired or dizzy, have a headache, or need to throw up. As the body gets used to the altitude, however, these problems usually go away.

People living in or visiting higher altitudes face other dangers as well. These threats include cold temperatures and **ultraviolet rays** from the sun. Ultraviolet rays can damage people's skin. They aren't as big of a problem at lower altitudes. The air is thicker there, which helps block them out.

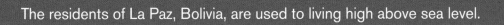

The residents of La Paz, Bolivia, are used to living high above sea level.

WHAT CAUSES ALTITUDE SICKNESS?

The human body needs oxygen to live. We get that oxygen from the air we breathe. The oxygen moves from our lungs to other parts of our body through our blood. If the body doesn't get enough oxygen, it has trouble working properly. When someone experiences altitude sickness, their body is saying it doesn't have enough oxygen.

Air is made up of many **molecules**. Besides oxygen, air includes other gases like nitrogen. About 21 percent of air molecules are oxygen. This is true everywhere on Earth. However, the air at higher altitudes is thinner. This means there are fewer molecules in each breath of air you take. It's still true that 21 percent of the molecules are oxygen. But since there are fewer molecules overall, there is less oxygen in every breath.

The thin air and rough, snowy landscape high in the mountains make it difficult for people and animals to live there.

Instead of talking about thick or thin air, scientists often talk about air pressure. Air pressure is a lot higher at sea level than at higher altitudes. More air pressure makes it easy for oxygen to travel from our lungs into our blood. Things are different at high altitudes. The air pressure on top of Mount Everest is 70 percent lower than at sea level. Lower air pressure means that people get a lot less oxygen when they breathe. That means less oxygen goes through their bodies.

Lack of oxygen is what causes altitude sickness. People get headaches. They lose their appetite. They have trouble sleeping. In serious cases, the brain can swell, or **fluids** can fill the lungs. Both of these conditions can lead to death.

Mount Everest

People climbing very high mountains stop and camp along the way. This lets them get used to the altitude as they go along.

GREAT ALTITUDE ADAPTERS

Altitude sickness and other high-altitude threats can be very dangerous. Even so, different groups of people have lived at high altitudes for thousands of years. For example, the Sherpas have lived in the Himalayas for about 6,000 years.

Scientists have compared Sherpas to people who live at lower altitudes. They have discovered that Sherpas have more red blood cells than other people. Red blood cells carry oxygen around the body. Having more red blood cells means the body gets more oxygen.

Scientists have also discovered that Sherpas have different muscle cells than people who live at lower altitudes. A Sherpa's muscles are better at changing oxygen into energy. Sherpas' bodies have adapted to make the most of the limited amount of oxygen available to them.

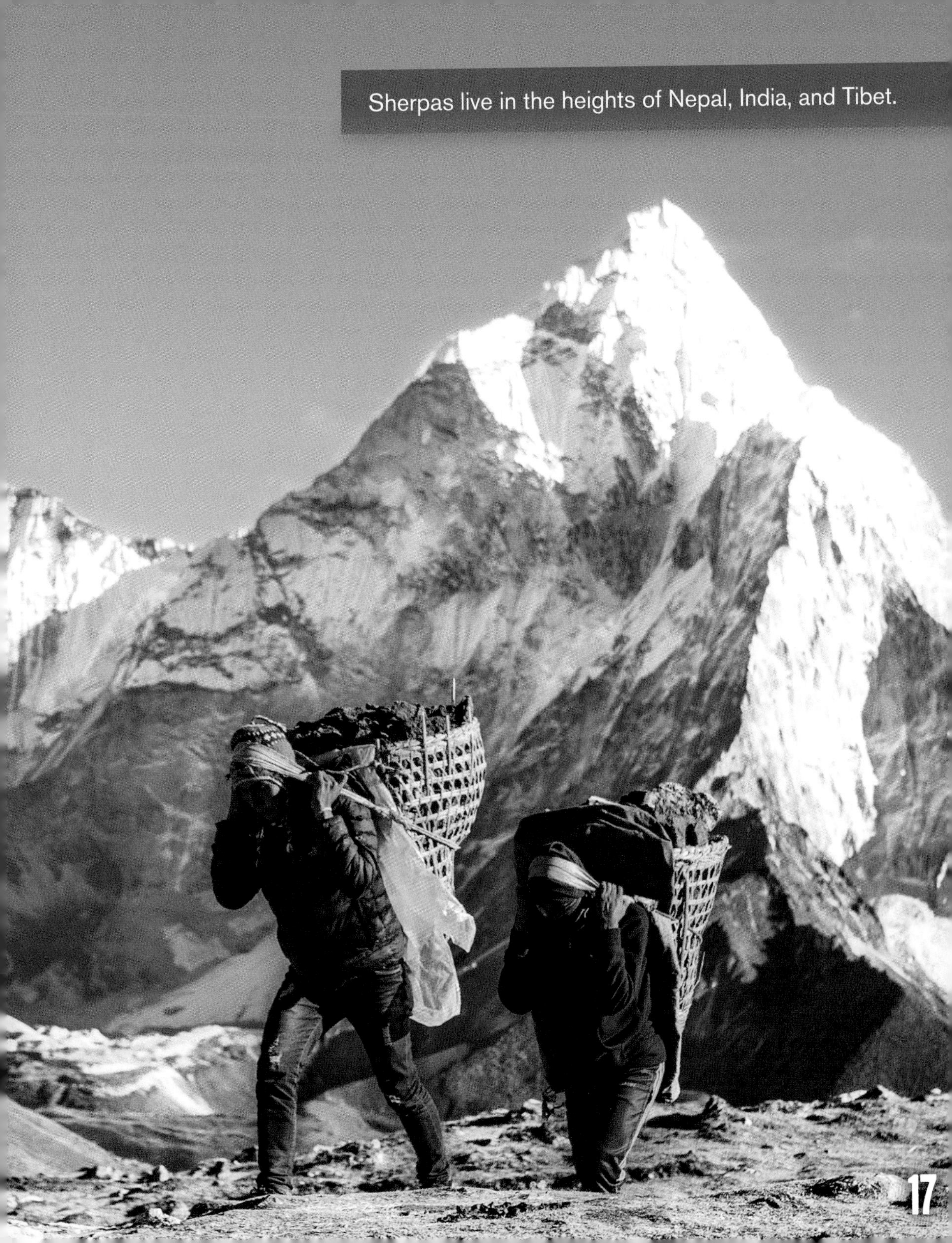

Sherpas live in the heights of Nepal, India, and Tibet.

Sherpas are not the only people who live at high altitudes. People have also lived high in the Andes Mountains of South America for thousands of years. Scientists have discovered these people also have blood cells and muscle cells adapted to life in the harsh environment.

When the first people came to live in high-altitude areas, they faced challenges from the weather, the ground, and the air. However, they learned to survive. They used fire to heat their homes and cook their food. There were plenty of rocks to make hunting weapons and other tools. People could travel to lower altitudes to find more food. Those who lived in the Andes also enjoyed hot springs and fresh mountain water. In time, they got used to the high altitudes.

Special Clothing

People who live at high altitudes need to protect themselves from the cold. In the past, ancient people made thick clothes out of animal **hides**. Animal hides also protected people from the sun. The sun's rays are much stronger higher up. They can easily cause sunburn. People had to cover their skin. Animal hides were a great way to do this. Today, people wear special suits, jackets, and other clothing to keep them safe, warm, and away from the danger of the sun.

The ancient Inca city of Machu Picchu was built in the Andes Mountains of Peru at an altitude of 7,710 feet (2,350 m).

LIFE AT HIGH ALTITUDES TODAY

High altitudes are exciting places. For a lot of people, they have a special kind of **appeal**. People choose to live at high altitudes for many reasons. Some enjoy the natural beauty. The air at high altitudes has less pollution than air at lower altitudes. That makes the air crisp, clean, and refreshing.

High altitudes can also be good for your health. People who live at high altitudes have better heart health. Their bones are stronger. Altitude also affects the appetite. Studies have found that people who live high up are less likely to be overweight.

At Work in the Air

Some people find special jobs in high places. The mountains of the western United States are home to shepherds. People from Peru, Spain, and other countries around the world have come to the American West to live in the high mountains and take care of sheep or cows. They live difficult lives but also have beautiful places to call home. Other people help visitors enjoy high altitudes. They assist mountain climbers or work at ski resorts.

A flock of sheep graze in a mountain field in Colorado. Shepherds also live in the mountains and look after the sheep, despite the harsh conditions.

Today, more than 140 million people live at high altitudes. There are many large cities in high places. Living in these places creates special challenges, but people have found clever solutions to these problems.

El Alto, Bolivia, is the highest major city in the world. It sits 13,615 feet (4,150 m) above sea level. It is located just above another large city, La Paz. The streets in La Paz and El Alto are narrow and steep. City planners had to think of easier ways for people to travel up and down the hills. In 2014, the government opened a cable car system to help people get around.

The steep slopes around La Paz and El Alto make growing food difficult. Many Bolivian farmers use a method called **terrace farming**, in which a mountain slope is carved into a series of flat areas that move like steps up the mountain. Some of these terraces are thousands of years old.

Estadio Olímpico Atahualpa in Quito, Ecuador

Cable cars carry people up and down the 1,640 feet (500 m) between El Alto and La Paz.

Athletics Up High

The thin air at high altitudes can do great things once someone has adjusted. This is especially true for athletes. Many athletes train at high altitudes. Doing this increases the red blood cells in their bodies. These cells can carry more oxygen. That makes athletes stronger and faster. Ecuador's national soccer team plays in Quito, which is 9,350 feet (2,850 m) above sea level. The high altitude gives the players a better chance against athletes from other countries, who might not practice in those conditions.

EVERYDAY PROBLEMS

One simple job that is harder high up is cooking. Lower air pressure means water boils at a lower temperature than it does at sea level. It may sound great that you don't have to wait as long for water to boil, but it isn't. The boiling water isn't as hot, so it isn't as good at cooking food. Pasta, rice, and other foods take longer to prepare at high altitudes. To get around this problem, people can use special pots called pressure cookers. They create extra pressure to help speed up the cooking time. There are also special cookbooks and food websites that change recipes so they will work better at high altitudes.

Baking is also different. Bread dough rises faster when there is less air pressure. Baked goods like cakes can **collapse** if they rise too fast.

In addition to cooking food quicker, pressure cookers keep food from getting too dry. ➡

TECHNOLOGY TO THE RESCUE

People who live at high altitudes have found some high-tech ways to deal with the lower air pressure. Some **residents** in the mountains of Colorado and Utah put special systems inside their homes. These systems raise the air pressure inside one room, or even the whole house. Increasing the air pressure makes it easier to breathe. There is no danger of altitude sickness. This is especially helpful for visitors. They don't have to wait for their bodies to adjust to the high altitude.

People who climb the world's highest mountains breathe through masks hooked up to oxygen tanks as they get higher up. The oxygen tanks have to be carried up the mountain, so they are designed to be as light as possible. Almost nobody climbs to the top of Mount Everest without this technology.

Most people who climb Mount Everest usually start using oxygen tanks at around 23,000 feet (7,000 m).

THE CHANGING CLIMATE

Today, Earth's climate is changing. The average temperature of the planet is rising. Scientists believe climate change will have a particularly strong effect on places at high altitudes. Warmer temperatures may create violent storms or cause snow and ice to melt sooner. This could cause landslides and flooding, followed by **drought** once the snow and ice are gone. Also, as temperatures rise, animals from lower altitudes will move higher up to keep cool. This could upset the balance of life in high-altitude environments.

Even with these concerns, living at high altitudes can be a great experience. In the future, people who want a different way of life, or people looking for new opportunities, can live in high places. They will find a challenging and amazing life there. Would you like to live at a high altitude?

Avalanches are already a danger at high altitudes. Climate change could lead to even more of them. ⊢———➤

Keep It Clean!

People may like visiting or living at high altitudes. However, they can seriously damage the environment. Climbers who go to Mount Everest have left tons of garbage on the mountain. This garbage includes plastic, oxygen tanks, and even human waste. In May 2019, Nepal's government sent workers to the mountain to clean up more than 11 tons (10 metric tons) of garbage. Each visitor is also asked to bring down more than 17 pounds (8 kilograms) of garbage after their climb.

THE WORLD'S 10 HIGHEST CAPITAL CITIES

CITY	COUNTRY	ALTITUDE (FEET)	ALTITUDE (METERS)
La Paz	Bolivia	11,940	3,640
Quito	Ecuador	9,350	2,850
Thimphu	Bhutan	8,688	2,648
Bogotá	Colombia	8,612	2,625
Addis Ababa	Ethiopia	7,726	2,355
Asmara	Eritrea	7,628	2,325
Sanaa	Yemen	7,382	2,250
Mexico City	Mexico	7,350	2,240
Tehran	Iran	6,004	1,830
Nairobi	Kenya	5,889	1,795

GLOSSARY

adapt: To find ways to live in new conditions.

altitude: How high up something is compared to sea level, or the surface of the ocean.

appeal: A quality that makes something interesting or likeable.

collapse: To fall over.

drought: A lack of water.

fluid: A liquid.

hide: An animal skin.

molecule: The smallest possible amount of a substance, like oxygen or water.

peak: The top of a mountain.

range: A chain of mountains.

resident: A person who lives in a city, village, or country.

terrace farming: Planting crops at different levels on the side of a mountain or valley.

ultraviolet ray: A kind of light from the sun that can damage people's skin.

INDEX

WEBSITES

Due to the changing nature of Internet links, PowerKids Press has developed an online list of websites related to the subject of this book. This site is updated regularly. Please use this link to access the list:
www.powerkidslinks.com/hdylt/altitudes